Surviving Hurricane Andrew

by Sharon Franklin
illustrated by Pamela Anzalotti

Scott Foresman
is an imprint of

Glenview, Illinois • Boston, Massachusetts • Chandler, Arizona
Upper Saddle River, New Jersey

Every effort has been made to secure permission and provide appropriate credit for photographic material. The publisher deeply regrets any omission and pledges to correct errors called to its attention in subsequent editions.

Unless otherwise acknowledged, all photographs are the property of Scott Foresman, a division of Pearson Education.

Illustrations by Pamela Anzalotti

Opener: Getty Images; 5 NOAA; 7 NOAA; 10 Getty Images; 11 Stocktrek; 16 ©Comstock, Inc.

ISBN 13: 978-0-328-51652-0
ISBN 10:   0-328-51652-X

4 5 6 7 8 9 10 V0FL 15 14 13 12 11

Kyla saw the big white RV first. She jumped up and down like a pogo stick. Kyla's my little sister. She's always doing silly stuff that embarrasses me. But this time I couldn't really blame her. I was excited myself.

Grandma and Gramps were coming to visit. It was August and we hadn't seen them since December. My dad's a meteorologist—that means he studies the weather. He said he expected the weather to be perfect for their visit. Gramps would be able to take me fishing!

Before Grandma could get out of the RV, an orange
fuzz ball streaked past her. Kyla jumped up and down
again, yelling, "Scamp, Scamp! Come here!" Scamp is
our pet dog.

Mom and Grandma hugged, and Gramps told me
how much I'd grown. Then Dad's car turned into the
driveway. Mom ordered everyone inside for dinner.

During dinner Dad told us about a storm out over the ocean. Dad works in Miami, Florida, at the National Hurricane Center. His team makes hurricane forecasts. If a storm looks as if it will become a hurricane, the center warns people.

"Yes, this storm is a monster. It's called Tropical Storm Andrew. The hurricane hunter flew out and took a look at it," said Dad, "but we don't think it's going to turn into a hurricane. It doesn't look like it's headed toward land. We should have great weather this weekend."

Hurricane hunters are Air Force planes that fly over the ocean to look at storms.

Gramps cleared his throat. Nothing could stop Gramps once he got started on his hurricane stories. His stories are pretty exciting. Gramps and Grandma lived in Mississippi during one of the biggest hurricanes in the United States this century.

"Now Camille, that sounds like a nice lady's name, don't you think?" said Gramps. "Well, Hurricane Camille was no nice lady in my book. In 1969 she was a Category 5 hurricane. They don't get any worse than that. You wouldn't believe the destruction. Our house was a pile of broken toothpicks when Camille was done with it."

In 1969 Hurricane Camille destroyed homes in Louisiana, Mississippi, and Alabama.

After dinner, Grandma and Gramps were already yawning and looking sleepy. Mom said Kyla and I should get ready for bed too. Tomorrow was going to be a big day.

"We will have to wake up early, pack, and drive about thirty miles to the beach," she explained.

I kissed Grandma and Gramps good-night. Then I brushed my teeth and went to bed. I couldn't wait to go fishing.

Early Saturday morning we drove to our favorite fishing spot. It's right on the beach. It has a stream for fishing and is protected by a little sand spit. The sand spit helps make the waves smaller, so it is safer for people to swim.

Kyla and Scamp jumped out of the RV. Gramps and I grabbed the fishing poles and headed over to the water.

Gramps knows a lot about fishing. He taught me
to be patient and leave the line in the water for a long
time. He also taught me not to jerk the pole as soon as
I feel a bite. That's probably why I caught four fish.

Gramps has a special cooler for the fish. It's filled
with ice to keep the fish fresh. Soon Dad peeked into
the cooler and saw all our fish. He smiled at me and
said, "Look at that catch! We better pack up and get
back home so I can fry up these beauties."

Before I knew it we were back home. I followed Dad into the house. I noticed that the red light on the phone answering machine was blinking. Dad put down the fish cooler and punched the button.

"Roy, this is Emilio at work. Listen, Tropical Storm Andrew is moving right toward Miami. We can't figure out if he's going to turn north and back out to sea or not. We might be issuing a hurricane warning. The boss says we need everyone down here right away."

"Oh, my," Dad said, as he called Mom over. "I have to get down to the center. Andrew's headed this way. Gramps knows how to prepare the house, but you should head to the store and pick up extra food."

How A Hurricane Forms

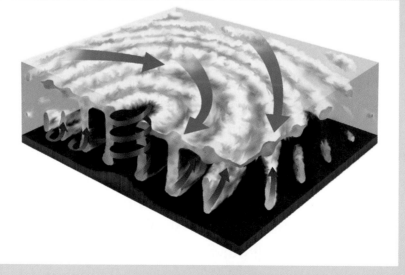

Warm air rises from the ocean. Then a thunderstorm develops. Strong winds form in the storm. When the winds swirl at 74 miles per hour or faster, the storm is called a hurricane.

Dad left immediately. Mom and Gramps went over a list of everything Mom needed to buy, including five rolls of duct tape.

Gramps told Mom he would fry the fish while she was gone. He turned on the TV just as the newscaster reported that they were now calling Andrew a hurricane. It was far out over the ocean, but it already had winds of 110 miles an hour. There was a diagram of a hurricane next to the newscaster's head.

The newscaster said, "Winds this strong can create a storm surge with tides as high as six to eight feet."

I gulped. I'm only four feet seven inches tall. I was glad Dad had decided to build our house inland.

This is a satellite image of Hurricane Andrew.

Mom returned from shopping just as Gramps finished cooking. He said it was too bad about Hurricane Andrew because Dad was going to miss some good fish. Gramps was right. The fish were great, but I was too uneasy to eat much.

Right after dinner, Gramps showed me what we were going to do with the duct tape. We needed to put Xs on all the windows so they wouldn't shatter in strong winds. Kyla was too young to help, but she tried anyway. I did the low parts, and Gramps put the tape up high. Then Kyla came along and pressed it on too, even though it was already pressed on fine.

After a day of fishing and taping windows, Kyla and I were ready to go to bed early. When I woke up on Sunday, it was still beautiful outside. The sun shone brightly. There wasn't even a breeze. I looked around for Dad, but Mom said he had only come home for a few hours before heading back to work.

All day we stayed in the house watching the news. The news people said everyone needed to be prepared for Andrew to hit land at any time. They showed more satellite pictures of the storm. Dad still wasn't back when I went to bed.

I think I was dreaming about fishing with Gramps when my door flew open. Gramps shouted that I needed to get up quickly and move into the hall.

Everyone else was already there, including Dad. Kyla was holding onto Mom and whimpering. I didn't blame her. I was pretty scared too. Scamp was barking at the whistling wind, so I picked him up and held him.

I could hear rain pounding on the roof and against the windows. The wind was howling and screeching. It sounded like trees were cracking, breaking, and falling outside. It was 5:30 Monday morning.

Gramps told us to try to sleep, but the noise made it hard. It felt like we were in the hall for days. Gramps said it had only been about four hours. Finally he and Dad got up and walked into the living room. They waved for the rest of us to come.

The hurricane was over. Through the window we could see the RV lying on its side. A big tree had fallen on top of it and smashed it.

As we walked outside, I thought about how lucky we were to have people in our family who knew what to do in a hurricane. I wondered what the night had been like for other people. But mostly I was glad that Hurricane Andrew was over!

Keeping Our Animal Friends Safe

During Hurricane Andrew thousands of families lost their pets. After the hurricane people formed groups to search for missing pets. Many pets were found and reunited with their owners, but hundreds of pets were lost.

Tips For Keeping Your Pets Safe

1. Your pets should always have identification tags on.
2. Prepare a disaster kit for each pet that includes food, medications, toys, a leash, and a copy of the pet's medical records. Also include a photo of the pet in case the pet becomes lost.
3. Have a pet carrier available that your pet can stand, lie down, and turn around in.
4. Talk to neighbors and friends, so they can take care of your pet if you can't get home before a storm.
5. Check with motels in the area to see if they will take pets if you must leave your home.